The People's H

A Nostalgic Look At Consett

by

The Derwentdale Local History Society

A group of Consett Iron Company apprentice electricians in the late 1950s.
Among them are: Steven Gailes, Derek McVickers and John Watson.

Previous page: Charles Harris nursing his pet chimpanzee 'Alex'. For many
years Mr Harris owned and managed a wild Animal Zoo at Elm Park near
Shotley Bridge.

Copyright © The Derwentdale Local History Society 2001

First published in 2001 by

The People's History Ltd
Suite 1
Byron House
Seaham Grange Business Park
Seaham
Co. Durham
SR7 0PY

ISBN 1 902527 28 3

Contents

Caricatures from Consett Iron Company's 'The Blast Personalities' of 1957.

Introduction

Since the foundation of the town of Consett during the mid-Victorian period, firstly as an iron manufactory and coal producer and later with the town and people's growth as a major steel manufacturer, much has happened.

Despite the many setbacks, of recessions and world wars and of the many subsequent social changes, that drawing together of the people of Consett in answer to a common call to overcome those difficulties are, in retrospect, very evident.

The history of Kings and Queens is only very partial. The real tangible history of our area is of our families, our industry and of our communities. This is critical to our understanding of not only today but also of our futures.

In an area which is so rich in history and of great scenic beauty, the benefits and fulfilment of research is also quite evident. This book, being the fourth produced by the Derwentdale Local History Society, brings together those threads of a society in which hard knocks and times have always been synonymous with life and is a testimony to a community's inbuilt resilience and capacity to develop.

So long as people believe in themselves and are mindful of that quotation 'Quo Vadis', or 'Where goest thou?', which is a reminder, both of our past and towards the future, then this pictorial record of the people of our area and of how they enjoy themselves, will serve to remind us well of the community in which we live.

Tommy Moore
For The Derwentdale Local History Society

Acknowledgements

While every effort has been made to contact and acknowledge due copyright within this book, the Derwentdale Local History Society would like to thank those copyright holders of photographs contained within the publication where this has not been possible.

Mr & Mrs Gerry& Greta Armstrong, Mrs Marion Barkus, Mrs Helen Cavanagh, Mr Alan Cox, Mr & Mrs Gordon & Norma Curtis, Consett, Blackhill & Shotley Amateur Players Society, Corus Group Ltd, Mr & Mrs Tom & Tina Davies, Derwentdale District Council, Mr Mal Edwards, Mrs Valerie Fairbrass, Mr John Gailes, Martin & Jeanette Harris, Mrs Vera Hewlett, Mrs Muriel Howe, Mr & Mrs Tommy & Norma Moore, Mrs Sallie Morgan, Miss Helen Murphy, Mr Joe Rayner, Mr Harry Rees, Mr Richie Smith, Mr Paul Starforth, Mr Teddy Taylor, Mrs Helen Wilson and Miss Joyce Wood.

Our Society would further care to thank those members of the general public who have kindly offered help and advice on much of the subject matter within this publication, without which some detail would have been sadly lost to future generations.

A few of our members on a visit to Gibside with the warden Mr Ken Gardner. Left to right: Greta Armstrong, Norma Moore, Tommy and Margaret Stephenson, Helen Wilson and Ken Gardner.

SECTION ONE

OUR YOUNGER DAYS

Consett Council School dancing lessons in the 1920s. Marie Noble, Marion Pearson, Murial Richardson are among the pupils taking part.

These pupils of English Martyrs were on a trip to Lourdes. Among them are: Helen Starforth, Elizabeth Storey and John Watson.

Consett Grammar School, 1937-38. Senior Mistress, Miss Wilson with Dorothy Brydon, Margaret Little, Elsie Ferguson, Ada Hutchinson, Vera Bird, Dorothy Bainbridge and Murial Richardson.

Teachers at Blackhill County Infants School in the 1960s. Included are: Miss Maude (Headmistress), Miss Ferguson and Miss Murphy.

Barry Kirkup, Barbara Mason, Janet Clark, Sandra Lamb and Michael McPherson among others in the dancing class at Shotley Bridge School in the 1960s.

Pupils having a singing lesson at Shotley Bridge School around 1960. Their teacher was Mrs M. Howe.

Pupils at Blackhill County Infants School's Christmas Party with Miss H. Murphy and Miss Maude in the mid 1960s.

Youngsters from St Mary's Infant and Junior School with Mrs Armstrong on an outing to Raby Castle.

Blackhill County Infants pupils in 1970 include: Thomas Moore, Graham Errington, Ian Watson, Judith Randall, Helen Mills, John Peacock, Gillian Robson and Malcolm Cowan.

Pupils of St Bedes' School in the early 1970s. Among the girls are: Anne Armstrong, Moya Mullholland and Allison McClean.

A group of young boys of Medomsley Cottage Homes with their house-mistress in the 1950s.

Miss Coates with children from Laburnum Cottage, Medomsley Cottage Homes in the 1950s.

Mr Richard Coombes, teacher at Benfieldside Junior School with the 1974 prizewinners. Among them were: G. Ferguson, A. Jack, D. Dalkin, R. Dodds, K. Walton, J. Hunt, P. Jenkins, A. Cranney, W. Bullawell, G. McPherson, D. Lee, J. Peacock, I. Colburn, A. Crane, C. Adamson, A. Morpeth, K. Armstrong, A. Marshall, F. Richardson, C. Davison, C. Marshall, C. Beatty, J. Turnbull and R. Turnbull.

Headmaster and teachers at Benfieldside Junior School in late Victorian times.

Ken Smith with Ronnie and Malcolm Nixon and friends in the early 1950s.

A lot of readers will remember this day in the 1950s. It was their 1st Holy Communion at St Patrick's Church, Consett.

Children at Moorside Sunday School.

Joan Gregson of Shotley Bridge – Girls' Athletic Champion, 1941, 1942 and 1943. Benfieldside School Headmaster, Mr Martin, presented the trophies.

The First Year Hockey Team at Neville's Cross College in 1940. Consett girl, Muriel Richardson is in the front row, extreme left.

An 18-year-old cadet in 1409 Consett Squadron, Frank Swainston, was presented with this cup. Flight Lieutenant Jack Harwood, Officer Commanding, is extreme right. The other boys include: Alan Fell, Tony Curran, Brian Murphy and Kevin Finnigan.

Consett lad, Paul Starforth with his swimming awards about 1953.

A party was held in Consett's Drill Hall for children of Consett Paras in 1964.

Leadgate County Junior School Football Team during the 1950s. Among those photographed are: K. Robinson (front row, second left) and Peter Brown (third from left).

A summer afternoon in the pool at Knitsley in 1959.

The River Derwent at Allansford has always been a very popular beauty spot on a summers day.

The Weir at Allansford, a popular swimming and bathing spot of yesteryear. Actually a head race to power the nearby corn mill during the eighteenth and nineteenth centuries, now a very desirable residential development.

A group of pupils from the new school at Moorside on a visit to Consett Iron Works.

A day at an air show at Church Fenton, Yorkshire, about 1984. John Moore, Justin Chilton, Paul McArdle, Richard Starforth and Stephen Lamb enjoy a brilliant day out.

A Christmas party for children of the Consett Iron Works Personnel Department employees.

A children's fancy dress competition at Castleside show in 1961.

Norman Bridgewater at Iveston taking part in the celebrations for the 1937 Coronation.

A group of friends gathered for Linda Armstrong's birthday in 1965. Included are: Marion Grimes, Kathleen Owens, Elsie Reilly, Anne Armstrong, Carol Day and of course Linda.

This group at Bridgehill in 1963 are: John and Janice Hope, Linda and Anne Armstrong, and Nigel Hope.

COMPETITION TIME

Derwent Valley Folk Dancing Team in the 1950s. Several Trophies were won at Darlington. Amongst those present were Miss Joyce Wood and Mr and Mrs Muir.

Jack Wilson, Medomsley Athlete with his cups in 1935.

Jimmy Brown (with gloves on left), welter-weight champion in the RAF, demonstrates his skills with Alan Walker at Consett Boys' Club.

Members of the Plate Mill Rifle Club 'A' and 'B' teams. Included are: Vic Thirlwell, Norman Boyd, Dennis Almond, Dickie Stirling, John Yager and Mr Tate (President).

Mr J. Hodgson, Superintendent of Templetown Brick Works, congratulates Ron Hall, inside forward for Consett Football Club, on the club's success in winning the Durham County Challenge Cup in 1959.

Happy days in Consett Baths with members of the CIC Swimming Club.

Whippet racing has always been a popular sport. Here are members of Derwent Whippet Club which met at Dipton.

Monday night was keep-fit night at Consett Technical College where Mr Fred Robinson was a very competent instructor well liked by all.

Consett Chess Club was founded in 1919 and here we find members watching a game between Mr Fred Fallows and Mr L.S. Freebury in 1959.

Finalists in the CIC inter-departmental darts contest way back in 1958. Pattern Shops were the winners. Included are: W. Lee (Captain), E. Jones, C. Capstick, C. Pooley, B. Chivers, A. Hewitt and J. Griffiths.

Darts winners in the CIC knock-out competitions in 1963 were the Masons Department with the Pattern Shops 'A' team the runners up.

Darts and dominoes men of the Slab, Bloom & Billet Mill receive their awards from Mr Norman Heaviside, Manager Fell Coke Works, in 1968.

The domino winners in the competition in 1963 were the Fell Coke Works (seated) with the Fitting Shop (standing) second.

The finals of the inter-departmental knock-out competitions in 1966, where the winners of the dominoes were the Masons 'B' with runners up the Boiler Shop. The competition was held in Blackfyne Pavilion and was watched by a keen audience.

These are both the billiards and snooker finalists of the CIC inter-departmental competition. Winners of billiards were Weighmen and runners up were Hownsgill. The snooker was won by Stores Control 'A' and runners up were Stores 'B'.

Taken in the Consett Billiards Rooms (now the Steel Club), Donald Cruikshank, former boy billiards champion, tells Consett lads the correct way to 'cue up' when he gave an exhibition.

Smiles from all at the final of the CIC winter table tennis games. Winners were the Blast Furnace Mechanics and losers were the General Offices. Chairman, Mr J.B. Bowie, is on the extreme right.

Fourth time lucky for the Masons 'A' Dominoes Team of Consett Iron Company in 1976. Featured are: Bill Harris, Marty McBride, Ron Garbutt, J. Robson, Bob Geddes, Chris Robson and J. Maughan.

Mrs Brenda Hume, wife of Bill Hume, Works Manager (Mills), seen here with referees of the inter-works 1974-75 Winter Sports Competitions at a social evening in the Consett Civic Hall. The referees were J. Cranston, R. Fail and A. Scott.

These young Consett ladies were all judo enthusiasts in 1962.

Members of CIC Judo Club after a weekend of coaching sessions at the Fell Canteen.

Two champion judo men, Mr E. Eastham and Mr W. Thompson, came back home with black belts after attending a course at Chigwell, Essex, in 1966.

Taking a break during coaching sessions, Eric Eastham and Charles Oughton and others.

Mr S. Bates, Chairman of Consett Golf Club, and Mrs Bates with junior members and families after playing for the Sydney Bates Trophy. Winner of the boys was David Atkinson and girls was Dorothy Askew.

A special exhibition charity match at Consett Golf Course attracted quite a lot of spectators when players were: Michael Bonallack (British Amateur Champion), Jim Baxter (Sunderland footballer), Alan Thirlwell (England & Gosforth) and Stan Anderson (Newcastle United).

A popular hobby in Consett in 1962 was the Company's Archery Club. Five members shown here are: A. Errington, S. Errington, A. Errington, B. Clough and K. Dilley.

This was the fifth annual club championships when Miss Pamela Raine became champion of the ladies' section with Mrs Molly Burns second.

The staff 3-legged race at the Consett Iron Company Sports Day in the late 1940s. Harry Rees (Old Plate Mill Manager) and Sid Unsworth (Manager Pattern Shops) are the third pair from the right.

Consett Iron Company Sports Day in 1948, with the Chairman of Sports Committee, Harry Rees (centre), saying a few words with Jimmy Middleton holding the programme. Harold Boot has his back to the camera.

The CIC third Sports Day Programme held on Saturday, 6th August 1949 at 2 pm.

Consett Iron Company Sports Day Awards – left to right: J. Middleton, Jay Iley, Harry Rees, Mrs Boot, Harold Boot (glasses) and Jack Croft.

Consett Iron Company Sports Day after the sports ground at Blackfyne was refurbished. Harry Rees recalls: 'We put in concrete pitches, with matting covers, and nets for cricket practice. Later the County came back and allocated matches to Consett in the Minor Counties. The Greens Research Committee came in our early days and gave us good advice. It was a very interesting time for Consett Sports.'

Durham County Mixed Doubles Badminton Team were inter-county winners in November 1953. The team included, (standing): Colin Hurd, Bob Hobday, Beverley Eccles. Seated are the ladies: Marjorie Oliver, Nan Allan and Esta Wilson. The three men were Blackhill lads and members of Blackhill Presbyterian Club.

Well known Consett businessman, Alan Cox, Durham County's Hard Courts Men's Doubles Champion in 1949 and Newcastle Open Singles Champion in 1952.

Durham County Tennis Team at Minehead in 1953. Back row: Alan Cox, O. Wrightson, G. Cass, W.K. Innes and H.F. Thomas. Front row: C.M. Parr, J. Victory (Captain), W.T. Anderson and T.R. Miles. G. Cass eventually became Sir Geoffrey Cass, President of the Lawn Tennis Association.

Another league championship for Shotley Bridge LTC. Back row: D. Eccles, E. Morgan, D. Tate and D. Scholey. Front row: A. Cox, K. Tate (Chairman) and T. Collinson.

The first County Veterans Tennis match, Durham vs Lancashire, 1st February 1981 at Sunderland. The captain was Alan Cox. Durham won 2-1.

Some caricatures first published in CIC magazines showing company personnel who were keen footballers in the 1950s.

A treasured photograph is that of Blackhill St Aidan's Soccer Team, with Canon Jenkin Jones second from the right.

THE FOOTBALLER

He wears a brightly-coloured shirt,
And loves to frolic in the dirt.
He hunts the ball with agile grace
And sometimes stops it with his face.

W.H.ELDER

Sometime ago, a local market trader, Mr Mal Edwards, offered to the Derwentdale Local History Society, an autograph book which had been produced by a relative who had been a prolific and skilled artist. Mr W.H. Elder, the author, originated in Middlesbrough but became a well known figure who lived in the Consett area for many years. The cartoons used within this publication are but the tip of an iceberg of the skilled depictions of the social and economic mores of the day. They are a credit to the author and we thank his family for their consideration in allowing us to use them within this book.

Here is W.H. Elder's view of football.

CIC's Sunday team win the cup. Included are: J. Davison, M. McBride, J. Dettmer, G. Williamson, G. Walls, P. Rogers, T. Lumley (Captain), J. Hope, C. Carr, J. Malpass, J. Walls and A. Lee. The two mascots were Masters Wall and Lumley.

Another cartoon from the pen of W.H. Elder.

THE LOVER'S RETURN

Farewell! Farewell! the damsel cried
We part for ever from to-day
For I can never be your bride.
So take your ring and go away
And thus they parted. Oh how sad!
The world then seemed so cold & drear;
And the maiden stifled many a sigh
And brushed away the trickling tear.

But the lover he returned ere long
And stood before her sad and pale;
"Please do not turn aside," He did
But listen dear one, to my tale
I went forth suffering from the pangs
And tortures of an anguished mind
But I've returned, for as you see,
I left my only 'gamp' behind

This was St Cuthbert's Church Soccer Team of long ago.

Hownsgill won the CIC inter-departmental cup when they played against the Offices in 1966. Mr J. McGillivray, General Works Manager, presented the cup to R. Gleghorn, captain of the winning team.

Consett Round Table Soap Box Derby at Mutton Clog in 1960. The boys, aged 12-15 years, raced in home-made bogies down a 200 yard track. The winners were 12-year-old Harry Bunny, 13-year-old George Ridley and 14-year-old David Stalley. The Obstacle Race was won by G. Gowland and E. McCance.

The Soap Box Derby, Mutton Clog in 1960.

Mr J.M. Jack presenting the trophy to M. Chester of the Fell 'B' team when they won the CIC inter-departmental bowls competition in Consett Park in 1959.

The teams line up for a contest between a CIC XV and Consett Rugby Club in 1961. The latter won 9-6. It was the first XV formed by Company men.

SECTION THREE

DAYS OF SUMMER

Buses lined up in Parliament Street to give the Consett Poor Children an outing to the seaside in 1923.

Passing through Burnopfield, the Consett Poor Children's Outing snakes its way towards the seaside in 1923.

A billing of 1895 advertising the Venture coach runs between Scarborough and Bridlington well before it ran in our locality.

Right and below: Men from Consett and Jarrow embarking for a cruise between the Cumbraes, Garroch Head Sound and Kyles of Bute. For the men who embarked there were many humorous moments.

A party from Consett Blast Furnaces visiting the iron ore quay at Tyne Dock.

Members of the Traffic Social Club as they set out for a visit to Vaux Brewery in Sunderland.

Retired traffic men for the CIC have a day out at Seaburn.

Above and right: A Consett Iron Company staff excursion in 1966 to Windermere and the Lakes.

Plate Mill veterans outside the Trade Union Memorial Hall ready for a run to Weardale.

A good time was had by all when the Fitting Shops went to Blackpool Illuminations about 1951.

A Steel Plant Social Club outing at Seaburn. This is the men's 50 yard dash in the sports held on the beach.

Butlins at Filey in 1947 and George and Ettie Richardson enjoy a holiday with friends, Josh and Freda Lamb.

The Moore family on holiday feeding the pigeons in Trafalgar Square around 1948.

Two of W.H. Elder's cartoons
illustrating holiday times.

Muriel Richardson with her parents on holiday in 1928 at South Shields.

These four ladies had an outing to Whitley Bay in September 1966. Outside and inside right are Mrs Armstrong and Mrs Chapman respectively.

Which one is 'Alice'? Friends at Blackpool Pleasure Beach: Joyce Storey, Anne McKenzie and Norma Moore.

Norma Curtiss and Helen Hope enjoy a day at Scarborough with their children Tracy, Paul and Susan.

Friends from Blackhill Community Centre enjoy a weekend in Blackpool.

Dave Armstrong, Derek Martin and Tommy Moore enjoying a day on
Widdybank Fell, Teesdale.

SOCIALS AND SPECIAL OCCASIONS

Having a good time at a Halloween Party in the Temperance Hall, Templar Street, Blackhill in 1955. Included are: Margaret Pickersgill, Mrs Ridley, Joyce Wood, Mrs Watson, Sylvia and Syd Page, and Mrs Burns.

Flags fly in Blackhill for the celebrations of hoisting the British flag in Pretoria, South Africa, on the 11th June 1900. This is the bottom of Park Road, note the now demolished Rose and Crown in the background.

This is Bessemer Street, Blackhill. Note the Railway Bridge at Blackhill Station in the background

Sieman Street (now Laburnum Avenue) flying the flags for victory in 1900.

A view of Cort Street, Blackhill in 1900 to mark the relief of Pretoria during the Boer War. The corner of St Aidan's Church Hall can be seen adjacent to St Aidan's Street.

A float going through Blackhill in celebration of the relief of Pretoria during the Boer War.

Great celebrations took place at Blackhill after the raising of the flag at Pretoria during the Boer War in 1900. Consett Iron Company's Brass Band took part in the celebrations.

Part of the procession from Iveston to Leadgate celebrating the 1937 Coronation of King George VI and Queen Elizabeth.

Part of the 1937 Coronation celebration procession from Iveston to Leadgate.

'Lady with baby' is Cyril Johnson – all part of the 1937 Coronation Festivities at Iveston.

Fancy Dress at Iveston on the occasion of the 1937 Coronation. Included are: Billy Joyce (man with the gun), J. Haggon, Eva Elliot (blacked up), Carrie Coulter, Mrs Kilpatrick (pointy hat), Mrs John Vine and Mrs Dobson.

Hamsteels Miners' New Lodge Banner, 1947.

Home on leave from the RAF to Roger Street is Bede Murphy with his parents, Mr and Mrs Murphy, and sisters, Nora and Helen.

Corontation celebrations at Bridgehill in 1953. Among the group are: Norma Hope, Mrs Murray, John Hope, Jimmy Bramwell, Audrey Scofield, Leslie Slaven, Eva Smith, Dorothy Hughes, Pauline Kennedy and sister, Peter Coleman, Mary Murray, Frank and Sheila Clark.

Consett's Hard of Hearing Club members in the cast of a play were: Syd Page, Mrs Pickersgill, Mrs Ridley, Miss J. Wood, M. Davison and Mr M.J. Burns.

A popular afternoon's entertainment at Consett Civic Centre was the tea dances seen here.

The draw for who was to take part in the Tyne Tees Television variety contest of 'Top Town'.

Top Town Stars – Derwent Valley Folk Dance Team were among the winners at the second audition to find Consett's 'Top Town' TV stars.

A Folk Dance Music Festival at Belle Vue Football Ground in the 1950s.

Derwent Valley Folk Dance Group at Belle Vue Ground during a music festival in the early 1950s.

Miss B. Entwhistle was presented with a wedding gift from CIC colleagues by Mr Hayes on the occasion of her marriage to Mr J. Devanney.

Mr Stan Smith (centre) celebrated his 21st birthday with a party in the Braes Hotel, Consett.

Mr Alec Roberts, BEM, of Durham Road, Leadgate, on the day he received his MBE from HM the Queen Mother in the 1963 New Years Honours List. On his left are Mr & Mrs Kevin Heweston and on his right are Mr & Mrs J. Roberts (his son and daughter-in-law).

Father Kennedy officiating at the Baptism of Kieran Armstrong McLean in St Mary's RC Church in 1992. Seen here with his proud parents, Anne Armstrong and Steve McClean.

The newly married Mr & Mrs Bede Murphy with their bridesmaids and best man, Mr Norman Starforth, brother-in-law to the groom. The bridesmaid on the left of the bride is the groom's sister, Miss Helen Murphy.

Miss Marjorie Hawthornthwaite of Leadgate marries her naval officer groom, Kingsley Barker, in the 1940s.

Miss Joan Farthing of Consett married Mr Bob Carson in the 1940s. The bridegroom, who was a policeman, was eventually promoted to Chief Constable. The father of the bride was chef to the staff at Consett Iron Company.

Above: On the
15th July 1961
Richard and
Elizabeth Smith
were married.
Included are: Mrs
M. Wright, Mr &
Mrs Jimmy Smith,
Miss G. Wilson,
Mr A. Thomas,
Mr J. Brown,
Mesdames M.
Smith, D. Pigg,
J. Potts, Mrs P.D.
Brown and Mr T.
Brown.

Right: W.H.
Elder's views on
marriage.

THE BLARNEY STONE

MARRIAGE

BEFORE   AFTER

A wedding at Carlisle Cathedral was the occasion for this photograph. Left to right, guests, Mr & Mrs Harry Rees with the bridegroom's mother Mrs Nave, wife of Mr Marshall Nave, a very well known and respected fellow in the Consett Iron Company.

Mr Frank B. George, MD Consett Iron Company, became President of the Iron and Steel Institute. The Annual Dinner of the Institute was held at the Grosvenor Hotel in London and seated about 1,000 guests. The Consett Iron Company was allowed two tables for Managerial and Sales Office Staff and guests. Harry Rees is seen front right.

In the 1960s and '70s Consett Iron Company put on a very good Christmas Dinner Dance for staff and officials at the Seaburn Hotel, Sunderland. This is one such dinner – left to right: Viscount Ridley (Chairman CIC), Mrs Allen, Mr Harry Rees, Lady Ridley, Mr Allen and Mrs Brenda Rees.

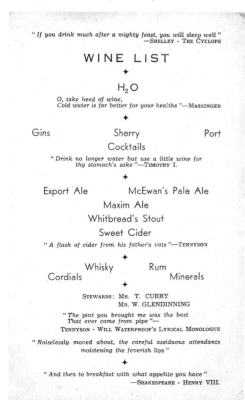

" If you drink much after a mighty feast, you will sleep well "
—SHELLEY - THE CYCLOPS

WINE LIST

✦

H₂O

O, take heed of wine,
Cold water is far better for your healths "—MASSINGER

✦

| Gins | Sherry | Port |

Cocktails

" Drink no longer water but use a little wine for
thy stomach's sake "—TIMOTHY I.

✦

Export Ale   McEwan's Pale Ale

Maxim Ale

Whitbread's Stout

Sweet Cider

" A flask of cider from his father's vats "—TENNYSON

✦

Whisky   Rum
Cordials   Minerals

✦

STEWARDS: MR. T. CURRY
MR. W. GLENDINNING

" The pint you brought me was the best
That ever came from pipe "—
TENNYSON - WILL WATERPROOF'S LYRICAL MONOLOGUE

" Noiselessly moved about, the careful assiduous attendants
moistening the feverish lips "

✦

" And then to breakfast with what appetite you have "
—SHAKESPEARE - HENRY VIII.

A wine list from a Consett Iron Company staff dinner in 1949.

C.I.C. PLATE MILL

Staff Dinner

THE CANTEEN

SATURDAY, 29th JANUARY, 1949

In the Plate Mills of the Company,
Ye who sometimes in your rambles
Through the broken bricks and shambles
Reach the Soaking Pits at last!
Here we heat the A's and B's,
Call for gas to get them hot,
Hope the chargers blow not up,
Hope the shears can cut the slabs!

From the neck of nine-foot six mill
Pluck we cobbles now and then.
Thro' the banks and to the shears
If in plate no crack appears!
Thro' the cold rolls of the Bay,
We are they who see the plates
For the orders from P. Benson,
Into wagons when we get them!
Send we plates by tens of thousands
To the waiting world outside.

AFTER - A LONG WAY AFTER,
LONGFELLOW'S SONG OF HIAWATHA

IN THE CHAIR   H. W. I. REES

A menu from the CIC Plate Mill staff dinner in 1949.

A happy occasion on the eve of her wedding, Miss Annette Davison has a get together with friends and colleagues to celebrate her forthcoming marriage to Mr Cyril Robson.

Everyone had a good time at the Broomhaugh Hotel in Riding Mill at the annual dinner of the Lubrication Department of CIC.

This annual dinner was for members of the Buying Department of the CIC in 1958.

A highly successful evening at the Freemasons Arms when Memory Man Mr Leslie Welch (centre) of radio and TV fame was in attendance. In front of him is Mrs Payne, Club Stewardess.

The first annual dinner dance for the Coke and Iron Production staff held in the Freemasons Arms, Consett, in 1960.

A happy group at the annual dinner for the Development Department of the CIC.

Members of the CIC Blacksmiths' Shop and their wives enjoying the annual departmental dinner.

An Autumn Ball for the Steel Plant Social Club was held in the Freemasons Arms in 1961.

The reception at Consett Gold Club annual dance. Pictured are: Mr Robin Williams (Club Secretary), Mr and Mrs Syd Unsworth and Mr and Mrs G.E. Ewan.

The Brick Works' social evening in 1968.

The Fitting Shop Social in 1968.

In the Fell Canteen the Savings Group Secretaries and friends held a very enjoyable social evening in 1959.

Templetown Engineers' social in 1968.

The CIC Telephone Operators had their social evening at the Bottom's Up night club in Consett in 1968.

The annual dinner of Northern General Transport at the Carlton Restaurant, Consett, 30th November 1967. Guests included: Mr and Mrs G. McCreach, Joyce Caster, Ronnie Ringer, Lance Green, Lena Mushgrove, Sammy Harris, Jennie Dowling, Mr and Mrs Richie Smith, Winston Lovett and Alan Gibson.

A social evening at the Carlton Restaurant in Consett with Sadie and Tommy Ayton, Mr and Mrs Jacky Walker, Greta and Gerry Armstrong, Honor and John Murray, Freda and Harry Brown and Winny and Billy Reilly.

Loading Bay Plate Mill Social Club.

A social evening for the Billet Mill at the Freemasons Arms, Consett. Included are: Tommy Heseltine, Derek McVickers, Terry McCabe, Derek Edgar, Jack Amos and John Sidey with their wives.

Shotley Bridge Tennis Club presentation night in the Carlton Restaurant. The Men's 1st Team was promoted to group 'A' Northumberland and Durham Tennis League in 1973.

This photograph was taken at Belle Vue Football Ground with members of the Derwent Valley Folk Dance Group during a Music Festival in the early 1950s.

A scene from a play by the Hard of Hearing Club who held their meetings and repertory productions in the Temperance Hall, Templar Street, Blackhill. These were always well attended and enjoyed in the 1950s and '60s.

A scene from the 1974 production of 'Viva Mexico' by the Consett, Blackhill & Shotley Amateur Players Society (CBS). Principal players were: C. Hume, D. Dawson, F. Boustead, L. Tones, M. Hall, A. McDonald, V. Gough, D. Hume, N. Lackenby, M. Sharp, A. Rose, D. Burdon and K. Little.

In 1956 the CBS presented 'Rose Marie'. In this scene are: Ruth Reed (playing the title role), with Lex Weatherburn (Sergeant Malone) and Derek Hume, Lewis Graham and Veda Ridley.

Another scene from 'Rose Marie' with Charles Laing, Elizabeth Milburn, Lloyd Matthews, Agnes Rose and Norman Campbell.

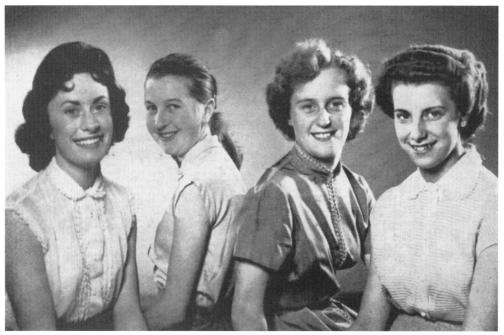

In the show 'Oklahoma' by the CBS in 1957 the dancers were: Winnie Robson, Valerie Ford, Glenda Robson and Valerie Sayers.

These young ladies were dancers in the CBS production of 'Oklahoma' in 1957:
Ada Morson, Irene Hannant, Marjorie Farnsworth and Joyce Bell.

When the CBS performed the 'Student Prince' in 1961 the part of 'Von-Asterberg' was played by Fred Boustead, 'Detliff' was John Huntley and 'Lucas' was played by Arthur McDonald.

Hamsterley Hall around 1890. This special occasion is somewhat obscure but the dress and formality of the occasion cannot be denied.

Junior Operatives of Consett Iron Company assemble at the Technical College ready for a course in Yorkshire.

An autumn hike from Bowlees in Teesdale to Cow Green Reservoir about 1985 saw Tommy Moore (Jnr), PC Dave Summers and Chris Dilly enjoying a brief respite from the rigours of the day.

1409 Squadron (ATC) at summer camp in 1988. Among those present were: John Moore, Ian Bland, Jay Frost, A. Anderson, 'Becky', D. Russell and D. Scott, to name but a few.

HRH Prince Charles meets some of the crowds who welcomed him on his visit to Consett in 1982.

Peter and Dot Balmer enjoying an evening 'hop' in Bournemouth in 1997.

SHOW TIME

The Consett Iron Company's leek growers included Vic Dent (fourth right) of the Slabbing Mill Leek Club in the Fountain Hotel, Consett, in 1968.

Mr F.B. George, Director and General Manager CIC, opening Consett's Annual Show in 1957. With him are: Coun J. Hunt, Chairman UDC, Mrs George, Coun Maddison, Mr T.W. Bell and Coun Woodhall.

Left: Mrs Pearson crowns the Consett Show Queen, Miss Anne Anderson in 1964.

Below: Mr Tommy Gaskill viewing the art exhibits by Consett Art Group at Consett Show.

Above: Malcolm McDonald and daughter Gail admiring some of the blooms.

Right: Austin Williamson gets his stall set up to aid Consett AFC.

Below: Ernie Aitkin, Vince Leadbitter and Eric Heaviside blowing up balloons for Consett Lions Club.

Above: Four young Consett girls wondering will the calf win a prize.

Left: Mrs M. Clark shows her winning exhibit to Miss Armstrong.

Norman Willis (second from right) watches a rifle demonstration on the cadet force stand.

Mr Frank McGurk (in white coat) former steelworker and licensee of The Smelters Arms, Castleside views the winning leeks at the CIC's Engineers Society Show which was held in the Smelters Arms in 1963.

The trials and tribulations of leek growing was illustrated in the CIC's magazine in 1968.

Mr Ronnie White (centre) winner of Consett Workmen's Club Leek Show. Club Chairman, Mr Tommy Walker is on the left and Leek Show Secretary, Mr Tommy Turner, is on the right.

Leek Shows were very popular as can be seen at The Victoria in Blackhill. Popularly known as 'Clydesdales' for many years, it is now known as the Derwentside Inn.

The Moorside Hotel Leek Show sponsored by Mr Bill Ferguson of the hotel.

Mr Holmes holding his leeks with Mr Tom Doolan, Steward of the British Legion Club, Consett.

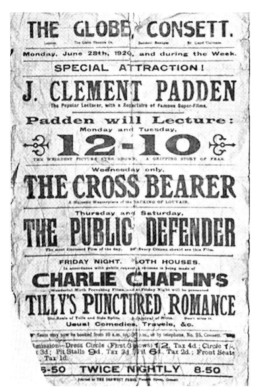

THE GLOBE, CONSETT.

Monday, June 28th, 1920, and during the Week.

SPECIAL ATTRACTION!

J. CLEMENT PADDEN

The Popular Lecturer, with a Repertoire of Famous Super-Films.

Padden will Lecture:

Monday and Tuesday,

12-10

THE WEIRDEST PICTURE EVER SHOWN. A GRIPPING STORY OF FEAR

Wednesday only,

THE CROSS BEARER

A Majestic Masterpiece of the SACKING OF LOUVAIN.

Thursday and Saturday,

THE PUBLIC DEFENDER

The most discussed Film of the day. Every Citizen should see this Film.

FRIDAY NIGHT. BOTH HOUSES.

In accordance with public request, a release is being made of

CHARLIE CHAPLIN'S

TILLY'S PUNCTURED ROMANCE

The Acme of Yells and Side Splits. A Carnival of Mirth. Don't miss it.

Usual Comedies, Travels, &c.

Seats may now be booked from 10 a.m. to 12 p.m., or by telephone, No. 95, Consett.

Admission—Dress Circle (First 3 shows) 1/2, Tax 4d ; Circle 1/-, 3d ; Pit Stalls 9d. Tax 3d ; Pit 6d. Tax 2d ; Front Seats, Tax 1d.

6-50   TWICE NIGHTLY   8-50

THE GLOBE, CONSETT.

Monday, July 28th, 1924, and during the Week.

STUPENDOUS ATTRACTIONS, THIS WEEK!

Special engagement at enormous expense of THE GREAT LITTLE

HACKENSCHMIDT

CHAMPION BANTAM-WEIGHT WRESTLER OF THE WORLD.

CHALLENGE TO THE WORLD

£500 £10

INTRODUCING HIS LATEST NOVELTY, THE UPROARIOUS COMEDY

GYMNASTIC WRESTLING HORSE

£10

RODEO · STUNTS · RODEO

Steer Wrestling Demonstration on Friday Night—

MAN VERSUS OXEN

Miss HETTIE MARSDEN, | Fred GREENY,

THE NOVERINES

CONTINENTAL NOVELTY ACT

WALLUS, | MASON & DORAN,

THE WORLD FAMED MYSTERY

SAXBYS

THE MOST BRILLIANT ILLUSIONISTS LIVING. A REVELATION IN MYSTERY & MERRIMENT

RODEO CHALLENGE GIVEN OUT NIGHTLY.   DON'T MISS MONDAY.

Seats may now be booked from 10 a.m. to 1-30 p.m., or by telephone, No. 95, Consett.

New Price—Including Tax—Dress Circle 1/6 ; Circle 1/2 ; Stalls 1/- ; Pit Stalls 8d ; Pit 5d.   Stall entrance adjoining Stage Door.

6-50   TWICE NIGHTLY   8-50

The Globe had top films on in 1920 when the Friday night star was Charlie Chaplin.

A different theme to show time at The Globe in 1924 with Hackenschmidt, champion bantam-weight.

Terry Sharp and Maureen Caswell win the pianoforte duet class at Consett Music Festival in 1961.

When Consett Grammar School Dramatic Society presented 'Hamlet', L. Lowes played the King of Denmark and Muriel Batey the Queen.

A scene from 'Hamlet'. Left to right: R. White (Marcellus), K. Fuller (Francisco), P. Hetherington (Horatio), M. Malpass (the ghost of Hamlet's father) and D. Stevenson (Barnardo).

A concert in aid of Oxfam raised £27 in 1964. The idea of helping Oxfam came from these girls: C. O'Hagan, P. Raine, J. Hewitt, M. Willis, P. Robson and S. Brown. The Escorts provided the music.

The Escorts offered harmony on many occasions – G. Booth, B. Clough, D. Reed and B. Armstrong.

Getting ready for sheep-shearing. A common sight on the farms around the Consett area before the Second World War.

Mr Joe Cole judges the children's class entries in the dog show at Belle Vue Park, Consett, in 1958.

CIC employees and families with their prize winning display at Consett's Chrysanthemum Society's Show.

Show time in the Melting Shop? A cartoon from the CIC's magazine in 1958.

Miss Avis Gilmour receiving the trophy for Chrysanthemums at the annual Consett Iron Company Show. Also included are: Mr G. Ewan, Mr & Mrs W.E. Ward, Mr Harry White, the show secretary and Fred Tate, show chairman.

Mrs Cole received a cup for best exhibit of floral art from Mrs M. Billings, wife of Admiral Billings of the CIC, at the Works' 7th Annual Exhibition.

Mr Forster was a proud man at a Leek Show held in the Trades Union Hall in 1968.

Winners in the Slabbing & Billet Mill Leek Club in 1965 were: 1st – V. Dent, 2nd – A. Bowery, 3rd – R. Owens, 4th – S. Robinson, 5th – G. Urwin and 6th – W. Renwick. One exhibitor was not present at the time this photograph was taken.

The Cole family have every reason to be proud when Mr Cole was first in the Flower Section at the CIC's Show held in Middle Street Methodist Church Hall.

Mr I.J. Skelton with his prize winning onions in the Company's Annual Show held in the Civic Hall, Consett in 1960.

Mr and Mrs Amos and Mr and Mrs Bowie examine the prize-winning blooms at the CIC Vegetable and Flower Show at Middle Street Methodist Hall, Consett, in 1965.

Several Company Departments ran their own Leek Shows, this was Hownsgill Plate Mill's in 1966.

At Consett Show there was always something for everyone to see in the CIC's marquee.

An advert for the CIC's Vegetable & Flower show. The Harold Boot Trophy for best exhibit in vegetable section went to Mr W. Snowdon (Steel Plant).

Mrs Kirkup presents E.W. Davison (Lubrication Dept) with the Mrs H. Boot
Trophy in 1968.

Mr and Mrs Kirkup with Mr and Mrs W. Snowdon, winners of the H. Boot
Trophy in Blackhill Community Centre in 1968.

THE END OF AN ERA

A double retirement presentation for Mr Sid Stobart and Mr John S. Ward of the CIC Fabrication Department, seen here with three of the younger tradesmen, David Hannen, Hilton Brown and Keven Brown.

Mr and Mrs S. Dent of Blackhill celebrate their Golden Wedding in 1957. Mr Dent who retired in 1951 was awarded the BEM in the 1952 New Year's Honours list.

Mr and Mrs J.H. English of Castleside celebrated their Golden Wedding in 1959. At the time Mr English enjoyed a 5 mile walk over the moors every day.

Mr and Mrs H. Ridgley of Blackhill celebrate their Golden Wedding in 1959.

Mr and Mrs Charles Stirling celebrate their Ruby Wedding anniversary in June 1957.

Total years of service for the CIC among these bowlers added up to 376 years. They include: J. Ward (55), G. Bramley (44), Mr G. Bell (53), Mr C.W. Sutton (18), A. Parry (42), M. Oliver (53), T. Borrow (27), R. Nevin (30) and W. Gardener (34) years service.

Mr Norman Heaviside had a double celebration on this occasion. Apart from receiving a gold watch for 35 years service with the Consett Iron Company from Mr Ward, General Managerit was also his birthday.

The Burns brothers, William and Albert, received their inscribed watches from Mr Ward, General Manager for their 35 years long service to CIC.

A presentation to Mr Alf Strand who having worked for 24 years as a chargehand fitter in the Blast Mechanics was promoted to a foreman's job at Hownsgill Mill. Pictured are: Mr and Mrs Strand and Mr and Mrs C. Hill.

Thought to be taken in the 1930s, these officials of the Consett Iron Company were on a visit to other works.

Daily walks are the best way to keep fit say these retired employees of CIC. They are: T. Nichol, K. Whitfield, B. Tindle, A. Maudlin and A. Storey.

Retired crane-drivers with officials of No 6 Branch, Bisakta (British Iron Steel And Kindred Trades Association).

They had a great day said the veterans of the Plate Mill having been to Hawick, Gretna Green, Carlisle and to a social club at Haltwhistle for entertainment.

Plate Mill veterans at their annual Christmas dinner in 1961.

Mr G.M. Nave, Consett Iron Company General Works Manager, Services, showing his watch to his family for long service.

A Christmas treat for retired men. Include are: J.R. Saxty, J.A. Thompson, F. Lowson, A. Dickenson, J. Watson, A. Downy, A. Barron, P. Hodgson, J. Gibson and E. Gardner. Each received a Christmas gift.

Mr R.R.L. Howe receiving a tribute for long service from Consett Iron Company Managing Director, Mr Pearson in 1966.

A presentation was held in the Fountain Hotel to mark the retirement of Mrs Lizzie Calvert after 16 years of service with the CIC cleaners. A wallet of notes was presented along with a rose bowl on behalf of her colleagues in the Oxygen Steel Plant.

A social evening was held in the Trade Union Hall in 1962 to mark the occasion of the retirement of Mr Jack Hall after 22 years as a pattern maker in the Pattern Shops. He was presented with a wallet of notes by Mr Syd Unsworth.

Blacksmiths' Shop veterans at their annual dinner and dance in the Freemasons Arms, Consett, in 1963.

Mr John Greer at his retirement celebration with Mrs Greer and their family. He was presented with a coffee set and table. Mrs Greer was presented with a bouquet.

Veterans from the Billet Mill having a good night out in 1964.

February 1st 1962 was the evening of Miss Errington's retirement party after many years in the pay department of Consett Iron Company. Miss Errington is in the centre surrounded by friends and colleagues.

Boiler Shop veterans at their Annual Dinner, Christmas 1966.

Mr R.W. Ward, instrument mechanic, at his presentation night at the North Eastern Hotel in Blackhill. Having served his time with the Joicey Collieries of Beamish, he was one of seven who formed the instrument section of CIC in 1952.

At a presentation at Consett British Legion Club, Mr James Love hands Mr Reg Tyerman the men's appreciation for his services upon his retirement from the Templetown Brick Works in 1968.

Departmental personnel of the CIC Fabrication Department who, year in and year out, organised functions, competitions etc, to raise funds for the retired and sick members who would each receive a Christmas Box from their friends and fellow workers.

Mr and Mrs Spraggon at his retirement in 1957 after 51 years service to CIC.

Mr Tommy Hetherington retired on October 1957 after 45 years in the Pay Department of the CIC.

A party of old aged pensioners whose ages totalled 4,774 years left Consett for an outing to Seaburn in 1958. They comprised 70 members of Consett Reading Rooms now the Steel Club.

Fitting Shop presentation to Mr C. Harris on his retirement after 51 years. Having served in France during the First World War he is best remembered as a professional runner and in 1940 was responsible for Consett Boys' Club winning several boxing trophies.

In 1957 Jack Moody retires after more than 30 years as a bricklayer.

Bob Sedgwick had worked in the Water Department of the CIC before he retired as chargehand labourer when he reached 65 years of age. He had been a keen gardener and in his younger days enjoyed being a member of the old Casey Court Jazz Band.

Miss Olive A. Coupland receiving a silver tea service from Mr F. Parry when retiring after 36 years of service with CIC. Miss Coupland had been in charge of the National Insurance Section of the Pay Department.

The CIC Company Secretary, Mr F.S. Woodward, with Miss Ella Charlton on her retirement. Miss Charlton served the Company for 47 years. Many will remember her as having a wide range of interests, from the Scout Movement, Animal Welfare and the RSPCA – and Hospital visiting!

A presentation from the CIC crane drivers! After 51 years service Artie Stewartson was presented with a wallet of notes to mark the occasion in 1965.

Consett Royal British Legion was the venue for many retired employees when they had an afternoon and evening of entertainment in 1967.

Mr Burnhope of Villa Real retired after 39 years service. He was the second electrical apprentice to serve his time. Mr Burnhope started work with the CIC in 1926.

Also available from The People's History

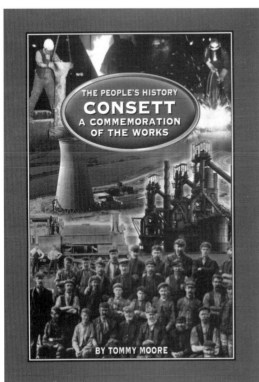

Charles Harris, a Fellow of the Royal Zoological Society, travelled throughout the world and is pictured here at Shotley Bridge Zoo at Elm Park with a Brahmin Bull about 1903.

The People's History

To receive a catalogue of our latest titles send a large SAE to:

The People's History
Suite 1
Byron House
Seaham Grange Business Park
Seaham
County Durham
SR7 0PY